GYMNASTICS
VAULTING
Tips, Rules, and Legendary Stars

by Tracy Nelson Maurer

Consultant:
Paige Roth
Region IV Xcel Chair
USA Gymnastics Women's Program
Owner Iowa Gym-Nest

CAPSTONE PRESS
a capstone imprint

Snap Books are published by Capstone Press,
1710 Roe Crest Drive, North Mankato, Minnesota 56003
www.mycapstone.com

Library of Congress Cataloging-in-Publication Data
Names: Maurer, Tracy, 1965- author.
Title: Vaulting : tips, rules, and legendary stars / by Tracy Nelson Maurer.
Description: North Mankato, Minnesota : Capstone Press, 2017. | Series:
    Snap books. Gymnastics. | Includes bibliographical references and index.
Identifiers: LCCN 2016001515| ISBN 9781515722212 (library binding) |
    ISBN 9781515722267 (ebook pdf)
Subjects: LCSH: Vaulting-horse—Juvenile literature.
Classification: LCC GV517 .M38 2017 | DDC 796.44/2—dc23
LC record available at http://lccn.loc.gov/2016001515

Editorial Credits
Gena Chester, editor
Bobbie Nuytten, designer
Kelly Garvin, media researcher
Tori Abraham, production specialist

Image Credits
Capstone Press: Karon Dubke, 7, 8, 10, 11, 14, 15, 16, 17, Martin
Bustamante, 22, 23; Getty Images/Jean-Loup Gautreau/AFP, 28;
iStockphoto: Brain McEntire, cover, 6, 18; Kelly Garvin, 20; Newscom: Ai
Wire Photo Service, 26, David C. Turnley/KRT, 27, David Eulitt/KRT, 19,
Jeff Siner/MCT, 25, Mike Blake/Reuters, 29; Shutterstock: Aspen Photo,
1, Brendan Howard, 12, ID1974, 13, Lilyana Vynogradova, 5, 21, Paolo
Bona, 9

Artistic Elements: Shutterstock: alexdndz, Hakki Arslan, kayannl

Special Thank You
Thank you to the coaches and gymnasts at GK Gymnastics.

Printed in the United States of America in North Mankato, Minnesota.
009686F16

Table of Contents

Leap Frog
with a Horse

Imagine a game of extreme leapfrog, and you're close to the thrill of the vault in gymnastics. To vault means to jump over something. Gymnasts use a **springboard** to launch their jump toward an **apparatus** called a horse or vaulting table. **Blocking** helps these gymnasts get big air—up to 8 feet (2.4 meters)—for spectacular tricks.

Vaulting is an artistic gymnastics event. Some artistic gymnastic events are for only men or women. For example, only women compete in balance beam and uneven bars. Men compete in still rings, pommel horse, high bar, and parallel bars. But both genders compete in vault and floor exercise events.

Gymnasts perform the vault with one or more moves in a fast series while in the air. Don't blink! The entire vault is over in seconds. But it can take months to learn a new move and even longer to polish the entire vault from start to finish. The amazing vaults at the Olympics begin with countless hours of practice and exercises.

Fast Fact:
Ancient Romans used a wooden horse to teach mounts and dismounts. Gymnastics borrowed this idea for the early vault apparatus, but today's vaulting table replaced this apparatus in 2001.

springboard—a strong, flexible board that is used for jumping very high
apparatus—equipment used in gymnastics, such as the vaulting table
block—a movement where the gymnast pushes off the vault table to gain distance and height for his or her move

CHAPTER 1

Ready, Set, Vault!

Vault practice should only be done at a gym or club with adult supervision. There, experienced coaches and the best equipment create a safe environment. In the United States, many clubs are affiliated with USA Gymnastics. Visit USA Gymnastics' official website to find clubs near you.

Vaulting work means sweaty practices at the gymnastics gym. A coach or trainer needs to stand nearby as a **spotter** every time you practice a vault. Spotters stay ready to protect a gymnast from a fall. Before you start doing skills on the block, you need to be prepared. And that includes showing up ready to work.

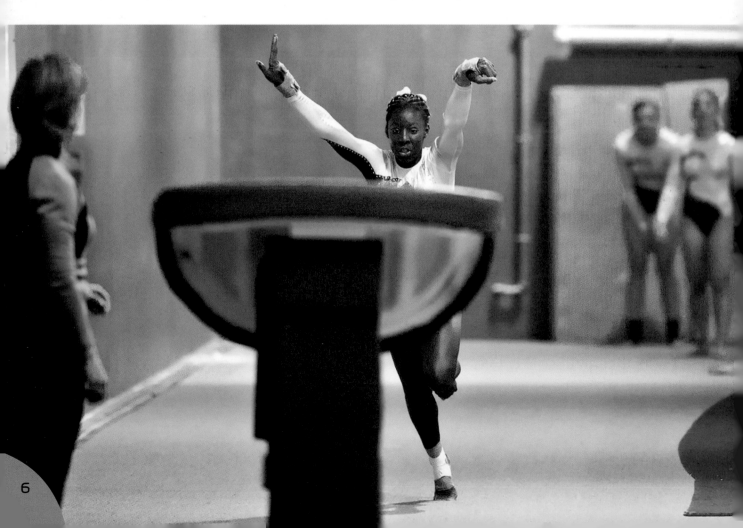

Gymnastics Garb

For training and competition, boys and girls must wear close-fitting clothing that won't catch on the apparatus. Girls wear one-piece stretchy suits called **leotards** for practice and competition.

For practice, girls may choose to wear spandex shorts with their leotards. They also pull their hair back in a ponytail or a high bun. Boys can wear shorts and T-shirts for practices. They also have the choice to dress as they would for competition. Boys compete in a **singlet** with short pants over it. Some wear short athletic shorts instead of pants over the singlet.

spotter—a person who keeps watch to help prevent injury
leotard—a snug, one-piece garment worn by gymnasts and dancers
singlet—a one-piece, sleeveless garment worn mostly by males for gymnastics, wrestling, and exercise

Table Talk

A vaulting table measures approximately 3.9 feet (120 centimeters) long by 3.1 feet (95 cm) wide for both men and women. The sloped front makes blocking safer for gymnasts. A padded surface absorbs shock to help avoid shoulder and wrist injuries. Women vault the table at approximately 4.1 feet high (125 cm). Men use it at 4.4 feet high (135 cm).

Preflight

Gymnasts practice running hard down the padded runway to gain **momentum.** Their knees pump high and elbows stay close to the body.

Gymnasts also work on their **hurdle** from the springboard to the table. They jump hard with both feet onto the springboard's surface to launch into the air. Some gymnasts perform a **round off** instead of a hurdle on to the board. Once they've landed the round off, they propel from the springboard toward the table using a back handspring.

The part of the vault from the springboard until the gymnast's hands reach the apparatus is called the **preflight**. Any preflight trick, such as the back handspring, should position the gymnast for the block. Hands come to the table flat and shoulder-width apart. The rest of the body aligns with the shoulders. Elbows stay straight. Ankles stay together in the preflight while the hands are in contact with the table.

Fast Fact:
Men have competed in the vault at the Olympics since 1896. Women began competing individually in the event in 1952.

momentum—the force or speed created by movement
hurdle—to run and jump onto the springboard
round off—a skill similar to a cartwheel but with both feet landing at the same time
preflight—the upward lift from the springboard toward the vault table

Postflight

From the block, the **postflight** shows off the gymnast's skills high in the air. Greater height from the block allows more time for tricks with complex twists and flips.

Landing

The vault ends with the landing. To stick the landing, feet should sink into the mat no more than shoulder-width apart. Bent knees absorb the impact. Arms straight out with palms down help add balance and prevent wobbling. Any additional steps lose points from judges. The gymnast immediately strikes a final pose with legs straight, back arched, chin up, and arms high.

Train For Speed And Power

Vaulting requires speed and power. A typical workout includes warm-ups, apparatus practice, and conditioning. Some conditioning workouts are:

- chin-ups, pull-ups, and push-ups to increase arm strength
- sit ups and planks that work the core muscles for tight flips and controlled landings
- plyometric jumps, such as small jumps on a mini-trampoline that build power and explosiveness for hurdles

CHAPTER 2

Block
Talk

Gymnasts strive for good form. They control every body movement so that their performances appear easy and graceful. They work on building powerful blocks and explosive launches from the table.

Fast Fact:
Gymnasts nicknamed the vaulting table "the tongue" for its curvy shape.

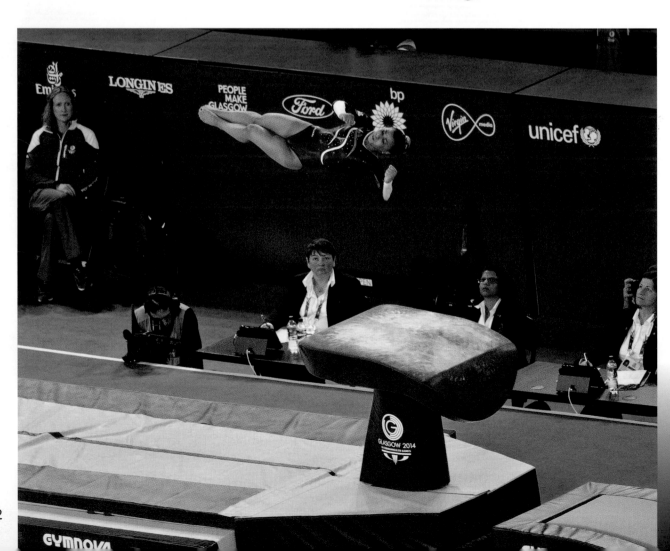

Judges watch the height or **amplitude** gymnasts reach from the table. The distance gymnasts propel away from the table also matters in competitions. If the judges think a gymnast's amplitude and distance aren't great enough, they will deduct points. How do gymnasts improve amplitude and distance? Practice, practice, practice!

amplitude—the height a gymnast reaches from a block off the vault

An experienced vault coach moves each gymnast step by step from basic skills toward difficult tricks. Skipping ahead to a harder trick before you're ready could stunt your confidence and, worse, cause injuries.

Fall Right

Every gymnast falls countless times when learning new skills. The trick is to fall safely. Practice safety rolls to absorb the impact of a fall. Roll in a tuck position in the direction you're already moving. Don't try to stop your momentum. Make sure your fingers don't catch and bend the wrong way. Cross your arms closely across your chest or put them over your head. Keep your chin down.

The Courage Vault

Coaches often start with this skill to help gymnasts fight fears of the vault. Jump hard onto the springboard and land feet first on the table in a tuck position. With knees up to your chest, jump off the table onto the mat. The goal is to practice good form throughout every part of the vault.

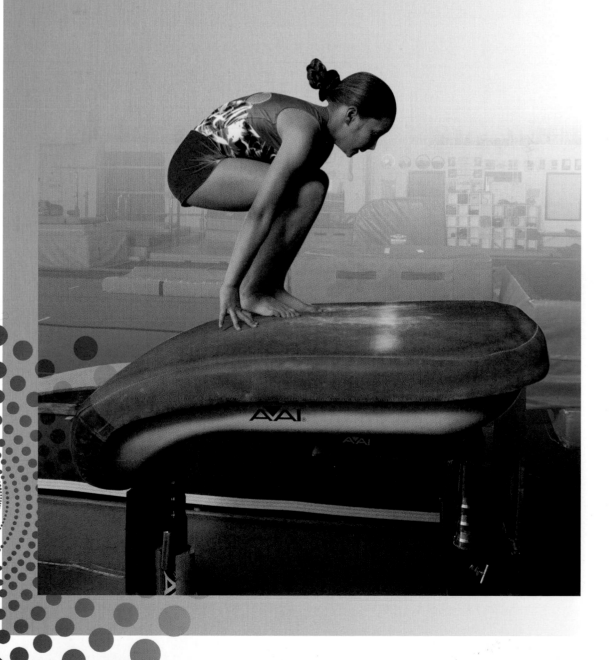

Learning new moves takes time. Think of the gymnast's body as making shapes like letters. Mastering these shapes sets the foundation for adding more difficult moves later.

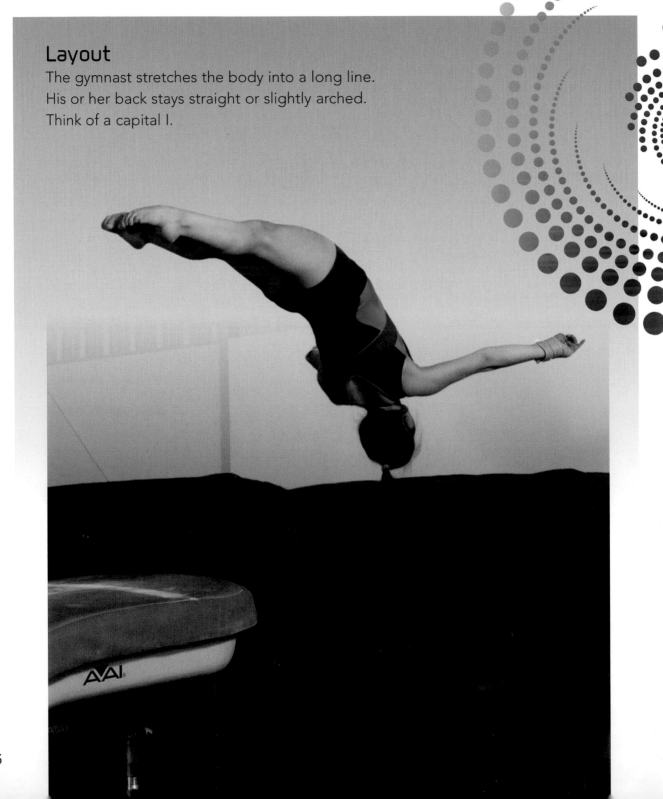

Layout

The gymnast stretches the body into a long line. His or her back stays straight or slightly arched. Think of a capital I.

Pike

The gymnast bends at the hips, stretching out the legs straight in front like a capital L.

Tuck

The gymnast tucks both legs up to the chest as if making an O.

The various skills and tricks in vaulting build from these basic letter positions. Just as cursive handwriting uses lines to connect letters, gymnasts add movements to link one position to another. Spins, twists, and flips add flair. And every gymnast gives his or her vault a touch of personal style.

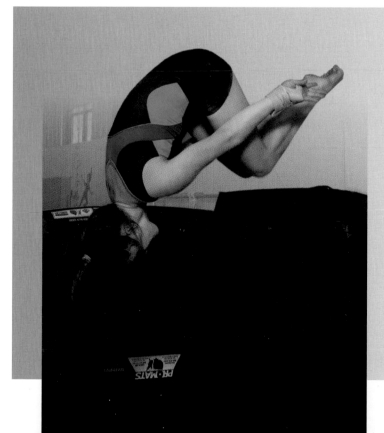

CHAPTER 3

Competition

It's important to choose a gymnastics club that fits your goals. USA Gymnastics offers the Xcel Program for less competitive-driven gymnasts. The program focuses on rewarding gymnastics experiences with fewer hours of training and competition than programs for Olympic hopefuls.

Gymnasts with dreams of the Olympics may compete in the Junior Olympic Program. The program has 10 levels and is run by USA Gymnastics. A gymnast must master certain requirements before he or she can move up levels. The top level is Elite. Once a gymnast is an elite, he or she may earn a spot on the National Team. Then the gymnast might be selected to join the Olympic team.

ATHENS 2004

*the 2004 United States Olympic team
after winning the team silver medal*

Gymnasts in levels 1-5 must master **compulsory** moves. Each gymnast performs the same skills exactly the same way. Junior Olympic levels 4 and 5 require gymnasts to perform a front handspring on the vault. Level 7 and higher can perform skills from the various vault styles in an official rule book called the Code of Points.

For Elite competitions, judges look at the difficulty of the vault (D score). Each skill has a difficulty value in the Code of Points. The sum of skill values equals the start value or D score. The judges watch the gymnast's form, amplitude, distance, and landing to evaluate execution (E score). Execution errors such as knees or ankles apart or extra steps on a landing are subtracted from 10. The remaining total is added with the D score to create a final score.

compulsory—a required element or routine

Competition Wear

Team members compete in matching uniforms. The Code of Points requires matching team track suits as well. They wear these during opening ceremonies, at the podium to receive a medal, and at closing ceremonies.

Women have specific clothing regulations for competitions. All girls must wear leotards that cover the stomach and back. Leotards should also cover undergarments.

Gymnasts risk losing points for wearing these items:

- T-shirt
- boxer shorts
- headband, cape, or scarf
- jewelry, although stud earrings are allowed
- straps less than 3/4 inch (2 cm) wide

Elite gymnasts often choose the skills with the highest difficulty points to increase their scores. The higher start value gives them a bit more room for losing execution points. Coaches guide their choice of skills so that gymnasts have the best chance of attaining the highest possible score.

The Olympics isn't the only place that awards medals. Top scorers at major competitions also earn medals. In these competitions, both male and female gymnasts perform just one vault run unless it's the individual or team finals. Then gymnasts show two vaults in a row. The average of the two runs determines the gymnast's final score.

Fast Fact:
A gymnast must land feet first to be scored for a vault.

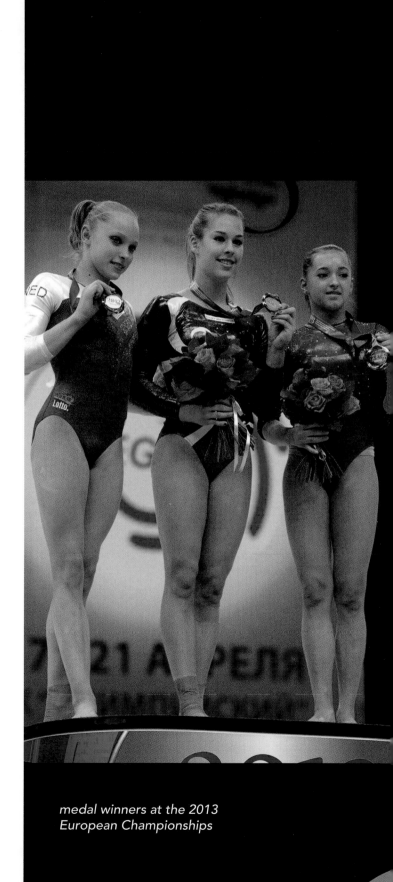

medal winners at the 2013 European Championships

Advanced Moves

Advanced gymnasts choose performance elements from the vault styles listed as categories in the Code of Points. The most common styles for both men and women include the Yamashita, Tsukahara, and Yurchenko.

The Yamashita Vault

Haruhiro Yamashita of Japan, a 1964 Olympic men's gold medalist, invented this vault. Gymnasts start with a straight hurdle from the springboard with a front handspring to the table. They pull up to a handstand when their hands reach the table for the block. Most Yamashita vaults feature a post-flight pike off the table. Like the other categories, this move has many variations.

The Tsukahara Vault (Tsuk)

This category is named for Mitsuo Tsukahara, a Japanese men's gymnast who competed in three Olympics. Mitsuo won a total of five gold medals from 1968 to 1976. His original vault in 1979 featured a quarter-twist handspring followed by a **salto** backwards in a tuck. Today most gymnasts do a half-twist pre-flight. Gymnasts need a strong jump off the springboard with a tall, tight layout. Gymnasts lift their arms forward and up to the ceiling as they lift and twist onto the table.

The Yurchenko Vault

Russian Natalia Yurchenko first performed this move in 1982. While completing this move, gymnasts have no view of the vault. This is called a blind-entry vault. Gymnasts first sprint down the runway and plant their hands onto a mat set ahead of the springboard. They flip their body into a round off and land both feet onto the springboard. Next they complete a back handspring onto the vault. From the block on the table, gymnasts can perform twists or saltos before sticking the landing. Today almost every Olympian performs some variation of this blind-entry vault during his or her career.

Names In The Code Of Points

The Fédération Internationale de Gymnastique (FIG) creates the Code of Points. Athletes' names are added into the Code of Points when they invent new skills. The skill must be demonstrated at either the Olympics or the Artistic Gymnastics World Championships. If FIG approves it, the group gives the skill the inventor's name in the next Code of Points. An updated rule book comes out every four years.

salto—a flip or roll

Competing Costs

Competing takes commitment from you and your family. An elite gymnast often trains 30 hours a week in the gym.

Coaches and parents expect gymnasts to manage their time well. But they know it's hard to balance gymnastics, school, and a social life. If you ever feel overwhelmed, find an adult you can talk to about pressures and expectations. Stay in contact with at least one person who is not in the sport. That way you have friendships and interests beyond the gym.

Competitive gymnasts are also responsible for making good decisions about health. They eat balanced meals with plenty of protein to build hard-working muscles. Eggs, spinach, cottage cheese, and low-fat meats are a few good choices. It's important to avoid skipping meals or following fad diets. This type of behavior is dangerous to the body, and can lead to an eating disorder. If you start to obsess over weight talk to your doctor.

Fast Fact:
Famous gymnasts such as Nadia Comaneci, Kathy Johnson, and Cathy Rigby have all battled eating disorders.

Prep Your Parents

Family and friends love to cheer for you at competitions. But even they have to follow competition rules. Every meet has its own rules. Some common ones are:

- no flash photography
- no food or drinks in the main gym area
- stay out of the competition area and off the equipment unless you're competing or a coach
- be respectful and professional observers
- never question a judge

CHAPTER 4

Legends
of the Vault

Gymnastics legends from all over the world have made the sport what it is today. These elite men and women inspire young gymnasts to pursue their own dreams on the vaulting table.

Mary Lou Retton

At the 1984 Los Angeles Olympics, Mary Lou Retton won a silver medal in the team competition and the vault. She also took bronze in the floor exercise and uneven bars. But she became an American gymnastics legend in the all-around competition.

First she earned a 10 on the all-around floor exercise, the best score possible then. But she was still trailing Romanian gymnast Ecaterina Szabo. She needed another perfect 10 on the vault to win. In seconds, Mary Lou wowed the world! She stuck the landing and became the first American woman ever to win a gold medal in gymnastics.

Fast Fact: Mary Lou Retton was the first woman on a Wheaties™ box.

Kerri Strug

At the 1992 Olympics in Spain, Kerri Strug was the youngest athlete in the Games. She won a team bronze medal there. Kerri struggled with injuries and multiple coaches for a few years after those Games. But she was determined to compete in the 1996 Olympics and earn high marks. She was especially confident on the vault.

By the last day of the Olympic gymnastics team competition in 1996, the Russians were in position to win the gold medal. On the first run, Kerri fell and hurt her ankle badly.

Kerri took her second run. She stuck the landing and saluted the judges on one foot before collapsing in pain. Kerri helped earn the American team a gold medal and became a worldwide star for her courage and team spirit.

Vitaly Scherbo

Vitaly Scherbo grew up in Minsk, Belarus. He loved gymnastics and trained hard for every event. He took the all-around silver at the 1991 World Championships, but he wanted to do better. He came back for the 1992 Olympics in Spain. There Vitaly won 6 out of a possible 8 gold medals in men's gymnastics, including the vault.

By the time he retired after the 1996 Olympics, Vitaly had won four more Olympic bronze medals. He also had earned 23 World Championship medals, including 12 gold medals. No one has earned more World Championship gold medals yet.

Fast Fact:
Vitaly Scherbo's full twist onto the vault is listed with his name among the more difficult skills in the Code of Points.

Yang Hak-seon

Yang Hak-seon's nickname is "the God of Vault." At the 2012 Olympic Games, he certainly earned the title.

In 2011 Hak-seon showcased a new vault he invented. The vault, FIG-named "the Yang," is a handspring into a triple twist. When he performed the vault at the 2012 Olympics, it had the highest D-score possible, a 7.4. The vault helped earn him the gold medal in the event.

Hak-seon had hoped to defend his vault title at the 2016 Olympic Games in Rio. He had even developed a new vault, named by fans as the Yang 2. Unfortunately, an Achilles injury in January prevented him from competing in the 2016 Games.

In addition to his Olympic appearance, Hak-seon won two World Championships in the vault event. He was also the first South Korean gymnast to win an Olympic gold medal.

Completing a vault routine takes a lot of hard work, dedication, and practice. Gymnastics legends have gone through it all and will inspire you to follow your own dreams. The vault event is a rewarding challenge for all gymnasts.

GLOSSARY

amplitude (AM-pluh-tood)—the height a gymnast reaches from a block off the vault.

apparatus (ap-uh-RAT-uhss)—equipment used in gymnastics, such as the vault table

block (BLOK)—a movement where the gymnast pushes off the vault table to gain distance and height for his or her move

compulsory (kuhm-PUHL-sur-ee)—a required element or routine

hurdle (HUR-duhl)—to run and jump onto the springboard

leotard (LEE-uh-tard)—a snug, one-piece garment worn by gymnasts and dancers

momentum (moh-MEN-tuhm)—the force or speed created by movement

postflight (POST-flite)—the upward lift from the block at the vault table

preflight (PREE-flite)—the upward lift from the springboard toward the vault table

round off (ROWND OFF)—a skill similar to a cartwheel but with both feet landing at the same time

salto (SAHL-toe)—a flip or roll

singlet (SING-let)—a one-piece, sleeveless garment worn mostly by males for gymnastics, wrestling, and exercise

spotter (SPOT-uhr)—a person who keeps watch to help prevent injury

springboard (SPRING-bord)—a strong, flexible board that is used for jumping very high

READ MORE

Carmichael, L.E. *The Science Behind Gymnastics.* Science of the Summer Olympics. North Mankato, Minn.: Capstone Press, 2016.

Savage, Jeff. *Top 25 Gymnastics Skills, Tips, and Tricks.* Berkeley Heights, NJ: Enslow, 2012.

Stanley, Glen F. and Ann Wesley. *Gymnastics: Girls Rocking It.* Title IX Rocks. New York: Rosen Publishing, 2016.

INTERNET SITES

FactHound offers a safe, fun way to find Internet sites related to this book. All of the sites on FactHound have been researched by our staff.

Here's all you do:

Visit *www.facthound.com*

Type in this code: 9781515722212

 Check out projects, games and lots more at
www.capstonekids.com

INDEX